MW01243365

My Words

My Thoughts

My Heart Songs

Terry Kelly Jones

UNFAZED PUBLISHING

TAMPA FLORIDA

ISBN: 9781959275299

LIBRARY OF CONGRESS : 2023912495

"For each petal on the shamrock, this brings a wish your way: Good health, good luck, and happiness for today and every day."

– Irish Blessing

UNFAZED PUBLISHING
YOUR MIND IS OUR BUSINESS

Dedication

To Erik

Christopher, Kelly and Jennie

Because of You I write Heart Songs.

My Words

My Thoughts

My Heart Songs

Terry Kelly Jones

My Words

My Thoughts

My Heart Songs

May the road rise to meet you

May the wind be at your back

May the sun shine warm upon your face,

The Rain falls soft upon your fields

And until we meet again,

May God hold you in the palm of His hand.

- Irish Blessing

My

Words

_____

Angel

She's my angel

She's mine to be with forever

I have prayed for such a woman of perfection

She radiates beauty and grace

All my prayers have been answered

Her voice, soft as a summers breeze whispers

and soothes my soul

her touch is a light

and as warm as a ray of sunshine

Her personality compliments my every mood

She never gets angry or judges me

She gives me faith and loves me unconditionally

Her face shines with joy and understanding

Her eyes see only purity and truth

She gives me strength with her presence

to beat all odds

Her smile sparkles like a star on a clear evening

She is perfection,

all the way down to her gossamer wings

For she is my guardian angel.

Lift Me Up

Lift me up

Let me soar.

Show me the way to serve.

To be with you evermore

I believe,

I have faith.

For you bring me joy

And everlasting peace.

Amazon's Christmas Boxes

Oh, Christmas tree

Oh, Christmas tree

All the gifts underneath I'm needing

Your lights reflecting on shiny paper

I don't have a lot of money

So half of them are just empty Amazon boxes

Oh, Christmas tree

Oh, Christmas tree

My secrets I hope you're keeping

For all the gifts I ordered last minute

just arrived today Dec 24th

Are now wrapped still in their Amazon boxes

Oh, Christmas tree

Oh, Christmas tree

It's now the day after our holiday

I'm happy but tired as can be

Because I waited so long to shop

Now I have to breakdown

all these dang Amazon boxes

The Poem

The poem that speaks of beauty

Love or hate,

Has only the thought of what has been said,

In many words and in many ways.

The expression,

The vastness,

And the understanding of the world,

Its beauty,

Love and hate.

It's joyous, not sad

Melancholy, not mad

Feeling, not numb

Understanding, not dumb

Living, not dying

Truthfully, not lying

Loving, not deceiving

Sharing, not surprising

Giving, not receiving

Creating, not deceiving.

Proclamation

Tomorrow I will

I will, I say.

Tomorrow I will diet but not today.

For today I have prepared a gourmet feast

Big enough to feed a very large beast and that's me!

So…

Tomorrow I will

I will, I say.

Tomorrow I will diet,

But NOT today!

Confusion is so Confusing!

Questions with no relevant answers

Dates having no specific time.

words blur on papers.

Poems that just won't rhyme

Confusion is so confusing.

There is no understanding of reality.

As simple as accepting and refusing.

Asking ourselves…. why me?

Misplacement of the little things

Trying to make things straight.

The loss of a thought when the phone rings

Trying to be early but always late.

Confusion is so confusing.

I seem unable to live another day.

It's my mind I am losing.

Somehow I'll make it through today!

Should I Try

I have an empty page with words

to be written upon it,

But what words?

How should I put them together?

What should I make them say?

Should they tell a story

about a person whose love was great?

Or should I tell of a person who was told to wait?

Should they speak of the words I Love You?

Should they speak of the sky

above whose color is blue?

The words of fear?

Or the sounds of a tear?

Of the man whose skin is white or brown?

Of the man's face who bears a smile or a frown?

What ideas should I speak of

and whose may they be?

Should I write a poets, or may they be from me?

When shall I write them, now or later in time?

Should I write them, should I make them rhyme?

Could I write them, could they be mine?

Shall I ask questions, should I pry?

I have but one more question,

Should I try?

You Are Forever Mine

You are forever mine dreams,

To last until the dawn breaks

And the glory of the day begins,

then creeps into the fantasies of you come true.

You are forever mine knowledge,

to lead me until I find my own way,

To depend on for all future uses and

to know what the true meaning is.

You are forever mine hope,

To think of what could have been and what will be,

The seconds of every minute of every day

to wait and pray.

You are forever mine faith,

To understand not only to believe,

God's creation, wondrous, joyful, mysterious

But fearful of the beginning and the end.

You are forever mine happiness,

To cheer even the bluest of days,

To drape pink and gold colors,

And bring forth an everlasting smile.

You are forever mine love,

To cherish and to need,

The give and the receive,

The warmth but not the jealousy,

the feelings of being loved.

You are forever mine world,

To plan for the future, to dream,

to lead and follow,

to think and wait

to believe and cherish everlasting.

Each is forever mine, young or old,

Each sunrise, every teardrop of the sky,

every child's laugh,

Every bright red balloon.

LIFE, you are…

Forever Mine.

May the raindrops fall lightly on your brow.

May the soft winds freshen your spirit.

May the sunshine brighten your heart

May the burdens of the day rest lightly upon you.

And may God enfold you in the mantle of His

love.

- Irish Blessing

School Is...

The house of learning,

A palace of thought,

A maze of numbers,

A path of sentences,

The place of scholars

Intellects and students

The property of the future lies within,

And led the past.

A social togetherness,

For learning of old and new ideologies,

The progress of success,

The failures,

The trials and tribulations,

The hopes and dreams,

Held within.

The silence and yearning,

People laughing,

Bells ringing,

people learning.

The movement of feet from a classroom

into the future.

The silence of the summer and

The new faces it brings,

Only to leave old images to memories,

A great strength of one to infinity,

And all that is worth believing is found in school.

Answers to Power

Dark, cold

It was not asked,

We were told.

Light, cool

It was recited.

We were the tool.

No, yes

It was taught to be done.

We were put to the test.

Questions, answers

Leaders led, powers the head.

Laymen spoke, no words were heard.

Backs turned; the people led.

You, me, we, us ... PEOPLE

Little sisters

Big brothers

High school buddies

College lovers

Friends in passing.

You, me, we, us ... PEOPLE.

Friends are .....

The eyes that hold a smile

The tear that lasts awhile

The thought of a happy day

The memory is kind this way.

The people who are loving and caring

The people who are receiving and sharing

The days of the present reflect the past.

The hope of one friendship that will last.

When No Man Dares.....

When no man dares to speak,

I shall preach my sermons.

When no man dare to enter darkness

I shall bring ray of sun.

When no man dares to laugh,

I shall bring joy to his heart.

When no man dares to walk alone

I shall walk and let him follow.

When no man dares to fill his heart with love,

I shall bring him a new heart to fill.

When no man dares to look upon his neighbor as a friend,

I shall be his friend.

Immigrant Families

From other lands they came to build their dreams,

They spoke no English, knew no words to say,

They worked hard and lived like peasants,

They were strong and forceful people.

They were the beginning of our nation,

They are the foundation of our world.

All the immigrants came here for a dream,

like their people did before them also.

To find their dreams and search for their riches,

these are people fighting to become one,

in a land so vast, dreams are found.

They come today, many years from the first,

And seek out the goodness our nation has.

For now we are a country, one and for all.

Freedom Fighters

Toll the bells, oh let them ring

In other lands let them sing

Oh, let them know across the seas

That America was founded for Liberty.

Free to be what we want to be

No tax on stamps, no tax on tea.

Let it be said that below the blue sky

It was done here they fought for freedom

'   "Freedom" they cried

It's here now that we're free men

That's the American pride

And it's here in America,

That the freedom fighters died.

Morning

This morning I was awoken

By a golden bespeckled

Ray of sunshine

Reflecting

In through my window.

The light grew lighter

As the day became longer

And the particles of dust

Continued their never-ending

Three minute waltz upon the air.

Upon reaching the window,

I drew aside the drapes

And looked upon an aqua blue sky with

Clouds of pink cotton candy,

Which were floating towards the ever

Vanishing stars.

A slight breeze stirred

The leaves on the

newly blossomed dogwood tree

that whispered the words to the tune

the blue jay sang.

As I began to turn away

I thought how lucky I was,

Then began my day.

Waiting

Waiting for the hours to pass

Wondering how long a minute will last

The slow ticking of the clock

Assures me that time is still turning

A new day will be dawning

Thoughts come back to me

I had tucked them away for some time

Wondering about things

Good and bad

All those questions forming

All the answers and still not knowing

Just waiting for the hours to pass

<u>Land of the Forgotten</u>

Land of the forgotten

>Do you exist?

Land of the forgotten

>Where are you among this mist?

Land of the forgotten

>Where do you lie?

Land of the forgotten

>Can you be seen from the sky?

Land of the forgotten

>Are you the future or the past?

Land of the forgotten

>Will man destroy you or will you last?

Land of the forgotten

>So beautiful are your lands.

Land of the forgotten

>God holds you in his hands.

Thoughts

_____

Sky

And the sky was dappled sky blue,

pink as golden white rays of sunshine broke

through the grey clouds.

In places and acted as a spotlight to the Texas

bluebells in bloom upon the carpet of emerald,

green grass.

An Autumn Eve

There is a frosted pink sky

on this warm autumn day.

As the sun dips and curtseys into the night.

Those last golden rays of the sun

That dapples itself upon

The last of the red, orange and yellow leaves.

Their gentle sway in the wind

is the start of a ballet only they have learned.

Thousands of years the trees have transformed

themselves into pirouettes of changing colors.

The last bow before dark

Seems to highlight fractionally the colors

and dance of a changing season.

Letting Go

Oh man

Here they come again,

the memories that keep my

heart breaking & the tears leaking

The thoughts of you frozen in time

I'm not ready to say good bye

I don't want you to leave

I'm not ready to let go

My life isn't going to be the same

There just isn't any way for you to remain

You've got a new path now

It's not going to include me

I've tried to achieve what you wanted me to be

I'm not ready to let you go

My life isn't going to be the same

There just isn't anyway for you to remain

Time isn't going to pass without thoughts of you

You still fill my mind with memories of happier days

I know we may never cross paths again but

I'm not ready to let go

My life isn't going to be the same

There just isn't any way for you to remain

Your time here with me was too short

Though years & years passed

I have to be honest & say the memories I've amassed

Will never surpass the life we had I'm sad to report

I'm not ready to let go

My life isn't going to be the same

There just isn't any way for you to remain

I've got to say goodbye I know

You'll be missed from this place we called home

Oh man, here they come again

The tears I always shed knowing you're no longer here

It's now just me & my memories

I'm not ready to let go

My life isn't going to be the same

There just isn't anyway for you to remain

A Rainy Day in NYC

Looking out from my skyscraper window

The fog and rain wrap itself around this city

I now see one where there was once two

A tribute to our freedom

Captured in the dewy morning light

Below the car lights are blurred

They look like clusters of spring dew flowers

Red and white, bright yet glossy

White on the right with red on the other side

Horns sound but from up here so high

They sound like a jazz horn out of tune

A simple & slight turn of my head brings another view

The Hudson with a bevy of tugs & ferries

The cloudy day makes the water a deep gray

No waves but from the boats plying their trade

In the distance another shore, another state

Glancing back again at the one that stands so tall

A memorial by its side,

a reminder of what shouldn't have been.

It's a city that will never forget

And now seeing this, being here

Neither will I.

When You

When you hurt, I hurt.

When you cry, I shed tears.

When you need me, I want to be there.

When you are happy, I am joyous.

When you smile, I smile along.

When you want me, I want you in return.

When we love, we share.

Dreaming

I once dreamed of castles,

And princes,

Of stately balls,

And cruises on the ocean.

Now I have my home,

My husband,

We dance alone,

And canoe on the lake.

Did I ever dream it to be any other way?

You For Me and Me For You

I know our love can't last forever

Like the rose, it must fade from existence

But the memory will last

All the good and bad times we endeavored

Will act as a strong resistance

For all the joy and pain of the past

And still we will continue on

As time ticks away

And painted pictures fade

Into our dreams from beyond

And those feelings that strayed

Are those that grew and stayed

I know our love can't last forever

But now is our eternity

Whatever the world contrives....is true

You for me and me for you.

Bless you and yours

As well as the cottage you live in.

May the roof overhead be well thatched

And those inside be well matched.

- Irish Blessing

So Far Away

He's there

I love him

But he doesn't know

Why or even how

Should I tell him?

He's only another man

But he's so special

His face, his soft lips

I wish for his to touch mine

To feel his arms around me

His hands to caress me

Oh, how can I love from so far away.

How?

I Don't Want To Say Goodbye

I don't want to say goodbye

That's not who I am

I can't stop the tears

And yet I can't accept you're gone

You meant the world to me

But now you'll just be a memory

I stare at your picture on my wall

And yet I can't accept you're gone

I'll never see your smile again

Never feel your warm loving hugs

Or see the smile in your eyes

And yet I can't accept you're gone

Where did the time go

How did all these years fly by

I kept in touch so much

And yet I can't accept you're gone

My heart hurts so much

My eyes won't stay dry

I know I don't have a choice

And yet I can't accept you're gone

Love you and always will

I know you are in a better place

Back together with your forever love

And yet I can't accept your gone

I don't want to say goodbye

You'll forever be in my heart

You will always be a hero in my eyes

I guess I have to accept you're gone

When the world seems to be coming at me

And the sun doesn't seem as bright

all I have to do is remember you love me

Then I know I'll be alright.

Always A Daddy's Girl

I miss you; I truly do.

I know it has been years, but I still want to share with you.

There are days where I know you are gone, that's nothing new

But I am a Daddy's Girl, and I have something to tell you.

I talk to you in my head all the time, but I still want to call.

I have to not pick up that phone, I have to stall.

Your grandkids are all grown up now, you'd be proud I am sure.

The power to write you a letter like always is still a powerful lure.

There are so many things that I have wanted to share with you over the years.

But I am a Daddy's Girl, so I still have many tears.

I think of you often, that for sure is true.

When I share stories about you, I still get blue.

I love you and still can't believe you are no longer here.

My love for you will always endear.

But I'm Daddy's girl what would you expect.

I am left with just memories now to recollect.

<u>Unsung Song</u>

Unheard songs

Of my heart

Playing melodies of songs

Never to be sung

Ballads of days past

Filled with forgotten lovers

Rain day songs

To cheer,

For friends,

To share,

To dream.

Songs of my heart

Unheard by others

For they are but words on paper

Never to be sung,

Except in my heart.

Good times, good friends, good health to
You and the luck of the Irish in all that you do.

- Irish Blessing

Falling

Falling,

falling,

down,

down,

from the sky, they come...

Falling.

teardrops, rain drops

dew drops lay

down,

down,

down,

to rest…

on the cheeks of a child,

the leaves of a tree,

on the petals of a rose.

Falling,

falling,

falling

down,

down from the sky…

Colors of India

The land of barren trees and holy rivers

the land of the forgotten past.

The land that asks come hither,

the land of colors of every caste.

The land of India is gold and green.

Gold the color of brass or the ripples of wheat,

the fields are not vast.

Green the color of the peacock's tail,

In full spread, traditions of the past.

The land of India is yellow and crimson.

Yellow is the color of its bright summer sun.

Crimson the color of the newly made bricks,

Used for the creation of a new building.

The land of India is silver and brown.

Silver the color of wares old and new,

Found in dark and dusty crevices.

Brown the color of eye showing pride

and offering their services.

The land of India is red and gray.

Red the color of Delhi's Purana Quila,

and other forts from India's history.

Gray the color of every dawn arising,

starting the new day with its old mystery.

The land of India is white and orange.

White the color of purity,

as beautiful as the Taj Mahal,

symbolizing honor and respect.

Orange the color of the setting day – dusk,

a color of the flag, and the hope of a new prospect.

The land of India is a rainbow.

Filling the skies during Diwali.

The land of India is pink

with the fat wild pigs running on the streets.

The land of India is violet,

the exploding colors of water balloons during Holi.

The land of India is turquoise,

the color of the sacred Ganges.

The land of India is its whisps of beige and the

and the burning of its beloved souls and holy cows.

The land of India is the assorted colors of its Dari's

And Ambassador cars.

The land of India in all of its colors can be

wonderful, dreadful, but always an experience.

The land of India is black, the color of death,

poverty and the ending of an old civilization.

<u>ALONE</u>

Alone,

Oh, so alone.

Time,

It passes by.

Thoughts,

linger into dreams.

Fantasies,

Just a simple wish.

Life,

A game to play.

Images,

Pieces of a puzzle.

Love,

Never being alone.

Terry Kelly Jones

I'm Growing Up

It's twelve o'clock and I'm home again

And I'm creeping up the stairs

I'm old enough but my Dad he really does care

I'm growing up

I just can't wait

I'm in a rush

I don't want to be late

The phone rings again

He calls my name

Says not to be too long

It's hard for him but now I've got to be strong

I'm growing up

I just can't wait

I'm in a rush

I don't want to be late

I'm not going to move out

not right away

we argue an awful lot

he wants me to stay

I'm growing up

I just can't wait

I'm in a rush

I don't want to be late

My

Heart

Songs

_____

Moments of a Lifetime

Leaning upon the doorway frame

I am bathed in a halo of light.

Coming from the hallway ceiling lamp

My eyes adjusting, I hear a squeak of

"I Love You"

"Shush," I whisper.

With arms stretched toward me

I bend over into a warm embrace.

Am I imaging this from my viewpoint?

Of myself as a child or

As me gazing upon my own daughter.

Our Desert Flower

Deep within the midst of the Mojave desert

Lives a plant of contradictions.

An ethereal bloom so delicate but strong to

Survive such a harsh environment…

A desert flower.

Like this floral beauty

We have seen you bloom.

Into a young woman, strong and willful too!

You have grown and flourished before our very eyes,

Our desert flower.

And now, "How big is JJ?"

So Big

A Child's Hand

Laid upon my arms, a gift.

A child, I smile and your small hand

Wrapped around my finger.

Together hand and hand

We giggled and wobbled a bit.

As you tried to stand

Entwined together we fit as one.

A butterfly fluttered and off you run.

Your hand slipped away.

As you turned away and said,

"Come play."

You held me tight by the hand.

Afraid I might let go, so brave.

You took that step towards the future.

I felt that hug in the squeeze of your hand,

Then you were gone

Today you took another,

mine together in prayer

that you should always know

that I would always be there.

Little Child At Play

Little child at play

Contented with the world around you

Find joy in the simplest of things

And the world will open its arms to you.

Beauty will surround you always

And there will be music in the air.

The world awaits you

And you will learn

That you have much to offer in return!

A Child's Forgiveness

A tear trickles down,

The peach skin of a child.

The ivory color streaked with

Strawberry red stains.

A frown grows,

from the cherry blossom smile.

The rose-colored pout glistens,

With tongue licked dew drops.

A quivering chin dances,

A simple waltz movement.

The innocent child's wrinkle,

Shows her sorrow,

And asks for forgiveness.

Child in The Summer Sun

Child in the summer sun,

playing in the wet sand.

He does not hear the symphonies.

He does not see the painter.

He does not see the sculpture.

He only cries

for his joy has been stolen

by a passing wave.

On Your Wedding Day

With **gratitude**,

I praise the Lord you were born my son.

With **joy**,

I watched you blossom as a boy into a man.

With **pride**,

I see what a caring, loving man you are now.

With **awe**,

I see and hear your work and it is amazing!

With **appreciation**,

for all the love you have given to me in your

lifetime.

With **love**,

my heart is bursting seeing you here, now starting

your family with your marriage with your wife.

With **honor**,

I accept your beautiful talented, smart and fun

choice of a wife.

With **thanks**,

you are the most wonderful, loving, considerate,

funny son any Mom would be proud of, but I was

blessed with you.

With **grace**,

I now relinquish my first place standing as the

most important woman in your life.

The love I see in your eyes, and the smiles I see

when you look at your wife, my dream for you to

have a happy life come true for you today as you

marry.

Did You Know?

Did you know that the stars are the only things that are as bright as your smile?

Did you know that my love for you is as tall as a tree can grow & touches the sky?

Did you know that your giggles can brighten my bluest of days?

Did you know that when you say "my Mom" that I am proud that I am your Mom?

Did you know when the world lets you down my heart hurts, but I extend my hand to lift you up?

Did you know I have kept silly memories about you because nobody else can share them except us two?

Did you know that my face muscles have gotten a workout over the years due to all the smiles you bring to me?

Did you know that I look at old pictures of you, so I never forget who you have been and who you are now?

Did you know you can brighten my day by calling and hearing your voice say, "Hi Mom"?

Did you know, though you tower over me in height, I match your height because I stand tall and proud of the person you have become?

Did you know I am sorry for all of the mistakes I have made with you over the years but so glad you have forgiven me for them, because I'm only human & not a super Mom?

Did you know that I still pray for you when you hurt because I can no longer kiss your boo boos away?

Did you know that when I am no longer here on earth I will always be with you?

Did you know that I love you?

Always,

Mom

You and I

When we met, I was still so young.

I didn't understand these feelings.

All I really knew was that I was happy.

I searched for you whenever I was near.

To catch a glimpse made my day.

I felt all these things I couldn't understand.

For I knew I had never felt them before

The first time you kissed me

my heart skipped a beat.

For some reason I felt light

I couldn't stay away; I just wanted you near.

You held my hand and we talked.

Like I had never talked to anyone before

And here decades later we still talk.

Your kisses still melt my heart.

I love touching your face softly.

It's a wonder that you are mine for always.

When we had to part for long periods

I would race to the mailbox every day.

Plus wait with bated breath for you to call.

I couldn't wait to see you.

And cried when you had to go.

When I finally got up the courage to say

I love you, darling.

You teased me & called me a silly girl.

The first time you told me you loved me;

I said say it again.

You have, every day, morning, noon & night.

You let me learn who I was & could be.

You have been there every step of the way.

You knew me, I told you the truth.

When you said you thought

it was time to get hitched

I stopped, took a moment

and thought of never having to say goodbye.

I never imagined being married.

Never dreamed of a husband, a house, a family

But I had to tell you my hardest truth.

If we got married I couldn't have children

I remember you held me while I cried,

and I felt safe.

I said yes,

that was the easiest decision I'd ever made.

We had to part for a while,

but I knew we were one.

The day we married

plays in my memories all the time.

Looking back now,

I know that was the most important day of my life.

We have had an amazing life together.

Ups and downs galore but we did it all together

I felt safe, we were and are still one.

When the good Lord blessed us with our children

I learned another kind of love.

A love that would keep them safe.

But we watched, marveled and laughed.

As our family grew from two to five

Even if our youngest took her time to arrive.

Our home was always filled with noise.

Some yelling but a heck of a lot more laughter

Together we raised three wonderful kids.

Who are now amazing adults.

There have been many times

my fears got the better of me.

Then you would hold me, I felt safe.

I'm amazed at the father you are.

This wonderful man by my side

You,

the man who says I look marvelous when I don't.

The same man who for the past 15,330 days

still says I love you.

You say it to me, and I believe you.

I know in my heart you do.

Just like all those years ago

when you said it for the first time.

We are back to just the two of us.

I couldn't love you more.

Yet every day I do, just a little bit.

When you kiss me I still melt

I love being in your arms.

I feel safe.

We still have a lot of time together.

And this new chapter of our lives

Will be wonderful.

Because I have you by my side

I love you; I respect you.

I thank you for loving me the way you do.

No matter how silly I get at times.

Your love has made me who I am.

May your blessings outnumber the shamrocks that grow and may trouble avoid you wherever you go.

- Irish Blessing

And Then There Was You .....

I grew up

I went out on my own

I met people

I made friends

And then there was you.

You came into my life

You changed me

You taught me

You shared yourself

And then there was love.

Forever and a day

Forever and a day

I will love you.

You alone

Have built

With me

A path

That leads

Into our future

Together.

Forever and a day

I will share with you

My joys

That you have given me.

Your Smile

I looked up into the midnight sky

And thought I saw your smile

But I was mistaken

For it was only a star

Without your sparkle.

Our Love

The wind whispered your name to me,

Though I did not always hear it.

The birds sang your song of love,

But I could not sing the tune.

Like the ocean waves,

you came to sweep me away,

I stayed like the solitary shell on the beach.

The sun shone your love upon my life,

Only tears like raindrops, did fall.

Now like time, natures full beauty is in bloom,

And so is our love.

Moms Always Say ...

Stand up tall,

Sit up straight,

Eat your peas, off that plate.

Don't get dirty, go out and play,

Please be good,

And obey.

Do your homework,

Don't do this,

when you're asleep,

It's total bliss.

You're too young,

You're too old,

but because you're bad,

I'm going to scold.

Go to sleep,

Get out of bed,

Move your bottom,

That's full of lead.

I'm older now,

No more pout,

Now I know,

I get to shout…

STAND UP TALL …

Our Time

Before my hourglass has emptied

And my time has come to an end

I want to as you just to remember

The times we have spent together

Besides just being a friend

You taught me what you knew

You brought new dimensions to my life

Helped me see myself as a woman

The lesson of love that I have learned

Was worth my effort all the time

And my memory box is full

Of mementos, dates, times and places

Time is slowly turning to an end now

And my poems don't rhyme anymore

You seemed to be there

When I needed you the most

Your boyish smile made me happy

Your tender kisses made me quiver

Your warm embraces made me secure

And though there are years between us

Our boundaries have been unlimited

And some of my dreams have come true

Slowly the last grains of sand drop

And my time has come to an end

The words I write with this pen

Are not all of the feelings I have

But besides the words I love you

And those are not enough

I want to say just two simple ones

And they are the best I can find

Thank You

My hourglass has emptied

Our time together has ended

And the grains of sand stand still

Like memories.

My Words

My Thoughts

My Heart Songs

Terry Kelly Jones

About The Author

Terry is a professional Travel Advisor, and it makes sense since she grew up traveling as the daughter of a US Government employee and diplomat. Growing up her family moved a lot due to her father's job, so much so she went to four elementary schools, three middle schools and four high schools. Sometimes she was only in one place for a few months and other times for just 2-4 years. From moving around a lot as a child in the 1960's and 1970's she formed a love of books and reading which eventually led her to writing creative short stories and poems. She contributes her love of writing poetry to a few of her middle school and high school teachers. One such school was the American Embassy School (AES) New Delhi,

India. There two of her teachers, Mr. Hurst and Mr. Pepperling made an extra effort in Terry's blooming creative writing and encouraged her to continue her writing in whatever form she enjoyed. It was Mr. Hurst who introduced Terry to the thought that the songs that we hear on the radio are just poems written to music. He had taught her and her classmates to listen to the Moody Blues to have them understand what he was saying, that poetry could take its place in many art forms.

As Terry grew up, married and started a family she started to write about her life, her family, her thoughts and more. She now finally understood Mr. Pepperling's phrase that 'poems are just your life's hearts songs.'

Book Terry

Email: TerryKellyJones.author@gmail.com

Facebook: Terry Kelly Jones

Please like and follow her.

Become an author.

Set up a free writing consultation today.

www.UnfazedPublishing.com

224.762.2242